D1714672

Compliments of

Gumdrop Books
800.821.7199

Great Scientific
Questions and the
Scientists Who
Answered Them™

HOW DO WE KNOW

ABOUT GENETICS

AND HEREDITY

JERI FREEDMAN

Great Scientific
Questions and the
Scientists Who
Answered Them™

HOW DO WE KNOW
ABOUT GENETICS
AND HEREDITY

THE ROSEN PUBLISHING GROUP, INC.
NEW YORK

Published in 2005 by The Rosen Publishing Group, Inc.
29 East 21st Street, New York, NY 10010

Copyright © 2005 by The Rosen Publishing Group

First Edition

Library of Congress Cataloging-in-Publication Data

Freedman, Jeri.
How do we know about genetics and heredity/by Jeri Freedman.
 p. cm.—(Great scientific questions and the scientists who
 answered them)
Summary: Traces the development of the science of genetics and heredity from Mendel to Watson and Crick, exploring how genes help determine individual traits.
Includes bibliographical references and index.
ISBN 1-4042-0074-6 (library binding)
1. Genetics—Juvenile literature. 2. Heredity—Juvenile literature.
[1. Genetics. 2. Heredity.]
I. Title. II. Series.
QH437.5.F746 2004
576.5—dc22

                                                      2003021817

Manufactured in the United States of America

Cover: Digital image of DNA bands
Cover inset: A model of DNA's double helix structure

Contents

The Beginning of Genetics

Why do we have the characteristics that we do? How are characteristics passed from one generation to the next? How can we improve plants, animals, and perhaps even ourselves? People have asked these questions from the earliest times.

More than 10,000 years ago, people recognized that characteristics of plants and animals

could be passed from one generation to the next. When prehistoric people first started growing crops, instead of merely gathering and eating the wild plants they found, they started to practice a primitive form of genetics. These early people planted wild species of plants. When the plants were harvested, people saved the seeds of those plants that had the most desirable characteristics, such as those that produced the largest fruit. Farmers also selected those animals with the most desirable traits and bred them. This process is so old that a reference to it appears in the Bible. In the book of Genesis, Jacob tells his father-in-law, Laban, that he will work as a shepherd for him and take as his pay all the black and spotted sheep and goats. Since most sheep are white, Laban agrees to Jacob's suggestion, thinking that he is getting a good deal. But Jacob, on the sly, arranges for Laban's white animals to mate with his black ones, producing increasing numbers of black and spotted animals, which he keeps. Eventually, Laban's family gets angry, and Jacob is forced to flee. This story

reveals that the basic idea that characteristics, or traits, could be passed from one animal to its offspring was already known thousands of years ago.

The method of breeding plants and animals to produce more desirable traits is called selective breeding, or artificial selection. It is the earliest form of genetic manipulation. In more modern times, the same type of selective breeding has been used to produce the various breeds of dogs, horses, and other animals that exist today.

Selective breeding was practiced by primitive farmers without any real idea of why or how traits were passed on from one plant or animal to another. As a result, the process was hit-or-miss. Sometimes crossbreeding two plants or animals produced a better offspring. Sometimes it didn't. And sometimes it produced results that were completely unexpected, such as a white lamb rather than a spotted lamb from two spotted sheep. So people began to ask questions. How are characteristics passed from parents to their

children? Why are some characteristics passed on but not others? Why can't different types of animals, such as cows and sheep, be crossbred? Is it possible to control which characteristics are passed from one generation to the next to get exactly the characteristics we want, instead of relying on the hit-or-miss method of breeding? Is there some basic unit of inheritance that carries characteristics from one generation to the next?

ANCIENT GREEK SCIENCE

The ancient Greeks were very interested in understanding the natural world and how and why things happened. They proposed a number of ideas about how the transmission of inherited characteristics took place. Pythagoras (c. 580–500 BC) believed that the male parent was responsible for determining the characteristics of the child through fluid collected from his body and that the female merely carried the child. Of course, this failed to explain why children often resembled their mother. This question led

Although Pythagoras's theories concerning inherited characteristics were incorrect, the great Greek thinker is considered the first pure mathematician.

Empedocles (c. 490–430 BC) to suggest that both the male and female parents produced material that went into making the child.

Hippocrates (c. 460–377 BC) is often considered the father of medicine. He thought that concentrated elements, which he called humors, were produced by different parts of the body and passed on to the child at the time of mating. This is called the pangenesis theory. Pangenesis means "created from many." Hippocrates also believed, however, that acquired traits could be

passed from parents to children. According to this idea, if a person built up big strong muscles, he could pass this characteristic on to his children. We now know that acquired traits cannot be passed on in this way.

The famous Greek philosopher Aristotle (384–322 BC) believed that when male and female fluids mixed at conception, "vital heat" was produced that cooked the new offspring into its final shape. Aristotle disagreed with Hippocrates about the transmission of acquired characteristics and attempted to disprove this idea by showing that parents who had lost limbs produced healthy, intact children. Aristotle proposed that the child actually inherited a "design" for its development rather than mysterious humors or elements. Most people at the time, however, dismissed this idea. Though they were not able to identify the mechanism by which characteristics were passed on from parents to children, the ancient Greeks were on the right track in looking for discrete trait-carrying elements that were responsible for this transmission. Unfortunately, during the Dark Ages, from about AD 500 to 1000, much of the wisdom of the ancient Greeks was unavailable to European scholars, most of whom spoke and read Latin but not Greek. During this period, research into natural phenomena continued at monasteries and early universities, but scholarly thinking was dominated by church doctrine, and for explanations people simply consulted what earlier authorities had said.

REAWAKENING THE SCIENTIFIC SPIRIT

The dawning of the Renaissance in the fifteenth century introduced a new spirit of scientific inquiry and a reawakening interest in studying phenomena by experimental methods and observation of nature. Our understanding of the natural world was about to change forever. The seventeenth century saw the rise of the first practitioners of this new objective approach, in which ancient authorities were rejected if what they said disagreed with observations and

measurements. More and more, scholars began to see nature, and even living organisms, in mechanistic terms, with parts designed to serve certain functions, like those of a machine. Scientific investigators, known then as natural philosophers, began to study the human body as a series of mechanical systems, and inheritance would eventually have to be explained in the same way.

William Harvey (1578–1657) was an English scientist born in the sixteenth century who is best known for explaining how blood circulates in the body. Harvey was born in Kent, England, in 1578. He graduated from Cambridge University and went on to study medicine at the University of Padua in Italy in the late 1590s. At that time, the University of Padua was the most famous medical school in the world. In 1602, Harvey received

English physician and anatomist William Harvey dispelled the belief that blood vessels contained air. He then went on to quantify the amount of blood in the human body before turning his attention to embryos.

his degree as a doctor of medicine. He became a physician at St. Bartholomew's Hospital in London in 1609 and was appointed Lumelian Lecturer at the College of Physicians in 1615, a post he held for forty years. In 1628, he published a book called *Exercitatio anatomica de motu cordis et sanguinis in animalibus* (Anatomical Essay on the Motion of the Heart and Blood in Animals), in which he explained how blood circulates in the body. But Harvey was interested in more than just blood circulation. He was also interested in embryology, the study of how embryos form. He studied the various stages that chicken embryos went through as they developed. Harvey found that embryos developed from eggs through a process called epigenesis. Epigenesis means that an embryo goes through a series of steps, developing increasingly specialized structures.

Because an understanding of how embryos form required studying very tiny structures, a real understanding of the process of embryonic development could not be achieved without a tool that would allow

Antonie van Leeuwenhoek, introduced to microscopy by Dutch mathematician and physicist Christian Huygens, first used microscopes to observe the quality of fabrics he sold.

researchers to clearly see structures too small to be examined with the naked eye alone. Antonie van Leeuwenhoek (1632–1723), a Dutch tradesman, would supply that tool. After working as a draper and wine tester, among other jobs, Leeuwenhoek learned to grind lenses and started to construct microscopes. Leeuwenhoek's microscopes were very simple compared with the microscopes of today. They consisted of a brass plate with a single magnifying lens mounted in it. A person

looked through the lens at a sample that was attached to a sharp prong that held it under the lens. Although Leeuwenhoek was not the first person to build a microscope, he was so skilled in lens grinding that his microscopes could magnify objects up to 200 times larger than when seen with the naked eye. With his microscopes, Leeuwenhoek was able to observe bacteria and other microscopic organisms, which he called "animacules." Among the microscopic organisms he observed and described were human sperm, which he identified as tiny living animals with tails.

In the wake of the realization that eggs and sperm played a role in the generation of embryos, there arose a school of thinkers known as the preformationists. Preformationists proposed that tiny, completely formed human beings existed within the sperm or eggs of the parents and that when a fertilized egg was implanted in the womb this little human being grew to full size. Among the early preformationists was the Dutch scientist Nicholas Hartsoeker, who in 1694 published a book titled *Essay de dioptrique* (An Essay on Optics). The book proposed that a tiny completely formed being, called a homunculus, was present in sperm. This concept continued to enjoy popularity for a hundred years. However, not all scientists of the day believed that the homunculus was to be found in sperm. Some, like the eighteenth-century Swiss scientist Charles Bonnet (1720–1793), proposed that the tiny humans were present in the female's eggs instead, and arguments between the two camps started to rage.

The Organization of Life

2

In the eighteenth century, two scientists set the stage for developing a clearer picture of inheritance. The first was Carolus Linnaeus (1707–1778). Linnaeus was born in a small town in southern Sweden. His father was a Lutheran pastor with a great love of gardening. Even as

Carolus Linnaeus, considered the father of taxonomy, restored the gardens at Uppsala University in Sweden, arranging plants according to his classification system.

a child, Linnaeus showed a great interest in plants. In 1727, Linnaeus enrolled in the University of Lund and later transferred to the University of Uppsala to study medicine. However, he spent most of his time collecting and studying plants. At the time, most medicines were created using plants, and collecting them was a normal part of medical education. However, Linnaeus's interest went beyond using plants for medical purposes. He developed the first systematic classification system for plants, categorizing unique species and

grouping individual species into larger related groups called genuses, orders, classes, and kingdoms. In 1731, he headed an expedition to Lapland, a region in northernmost Europe, to study plants and other nature-related phenomena, and subsequently he led several more expeditions.

In 1735, Linnaeus published the first edition of his classification system in a volume called *Systema naturae* (The System of Nature). In the decades that followed, he continued to expand this work into many volumes, classifying plants and animals from all over the world from botanists' samples he received. In his early work, Linnaeus believed that species were fixed and never changed. In his later years, however, having observed that different species of plants could crossbreed to form hybrids (plants that had the characteristics of different species), he altered this view and considered that hybridization could be a means by which new species arise. Although knowledge gained by later scientists has led to the rearrangement of Linnaeus's original scheme of

Baron Georges Cuvier was known for his accurate reconstruction of organisms from fossil fragments. He also established the extinction of organisms as fact.

classification, he is responsible for developing the first systematic approach to categorizing plants and animals. Other investigators, like the Frenchman Baron Georges Cuvier (1769–1832), studied the anatomy of organisms in terms of how they survived in their environment and began to compare the anatomy of living creatures to the features of dead ones preserved in fossils.

Another eighteenth-century scientist who moved forward our understanding of inheritance was Pierre de Maupertuis (1698–1759), a French astronomer and

mathematician. In addition to writing books on astronomy, he produced a number of works on biology. He noted that the offspring of animals had characteristics of both parents, and he proposed an early theory of evolution.

THE EVOLUTION OF SPECIES

There were many theories of evolution before Charles Darwin's theory. Darwin did not so much invent the idea of evolution as propose an explanation for how it occurred. The French naturalist Jean-Baptiste Lamarck (1744–1829) was one of the first scientists to suggest that new species of animals developed as the result of an evolutionary process. At the age of seventeen, after studying for some years at a school run by Jesuits at Amiens, Lamarck joined the army. Although he distinguished himself as a soldier, after eight years in the army an injury forced him to find a new career. Lamarck turned to the study of nature and medicine, and in 1778 he published his first book, *Flore Française* (The Plants of France).

Darwin credited Jean-Baptiste Lamarck (above) *as the first to propose that evolutionary changes were the result of nature and not miraculous.*

He was subsequently appointed an assistant at the Royal Botanical Garden, which was a center for the study of medicine as well as botany. When it was reorganized in 1793 to form the Museum of Natural History, he was appointed a professor there. In 1809, he wrote his most famous work, *Philosophie zoologique* (The Science of Animals).

Lamarck proposed that animals developed their present forms as the result of an extensive series of small changes that took place over a long period of time. Over time, changes in an animal's environment

produce corresponding changes in the animal's behavior, which in turn causes the animal to use some structures more and others less than in the past. Lamarck suggested that when a structure is used less, it atrophies, or shrinks, over a number of generations. He further proposed that such changes were inherited. We now know that acquired characteristics, traits acquired within the lifetime of a single organism, cannot be passed on from parents to their offspring. Because Lamarck supported the idea of the inheritance of acquired characteristics, his work is largely discredited today. However, his work is important in the history of evolution because of his suggestion that changes in animals take place gradually over time, an idea that influenced later evolutionary thinkers.

In 1830, the Scottish geologist Charles Lyell published a book called *Principles of Geology*. Lyell's book described evidence indicating that the world was much older than people believed. He challenged the idea that Earth had been created instantaneously by

God. Lyell proposed that it had attained its present state as the result of natural processes, such as wind and water erosion, volcanic eruptions, earthquakes, floods, glaciation, and other natural forces that had occurred over hundreds of millions of years. The idea that Earth itself was evolving, and that it was old enough so that small, incremental changes in new generations of species could accumulate and produce very great changes in the appearance or behavior of organisms, provided a solid, scientific foundation for a theory of biological evolution.

After a brief time at Edinburgh University, where he started out studying medicine, Charles Darwin (1809–1882) switched to Cambridge University, where he studied to be a clergyman. After completing his degree, he stayed on for a short time at Cambridge studying geology with Adam Sedgwick (1785–1873), and he accompanied him on a geological expedition to Wales. When they returned, Darwin received a letter from a friend, biology professor John Stevens Henslow

(1796–1861). The letter told him that a surveying expedition was about to be undertaken on a ship called the *Beagle* and suggested that Darwin apply for the position of naturalist with the expedition. On December 27, 1831, Darwin set off on an expedition that would last nearly five years, finally ending on October 2, 1836. What Darwin learned would forever change our understanding of how animals attained their present forms.

Darwin's primary area of study was originally geology. On the voyage, Darwin read Lyell's book on geology and was captivated by Lyell's theories about the age of Earth and the way it had formed over millions of years. He also read Thomas Malthus's *An Essay on the Principle of Population* (1798). This work claimed that population increases much more rapidly than resources, such as food, and that people must compete for these scarce resources. These two works would greatly influence Darwin later, when he sought to explain the variations he saw in animals on his voyage.

The *Beagle* first stopped at islands in the Atlantic Ocean, such as Cape Verde, and then proceeded to make stops along the South American coast and nearby islands, including the Galápagos Islands, located off the coast of Ecuador. There, Darwin found the evidence that formed the basis for his theories of evolution, in variations in the anatomical features of birds and other animals he observed. But he did not at first recognize the significance of his observations. The journey then continued through Tahiti, New Zealand, Australia, Tasmania, the Maldives, Mauritius, Saint Helena, Ascension, Brazil, and the Azores. When he returned, Darwin published an account of his observations in a book called *Journal of a Naturalist*. It was a number of years before he began to understand the process that was creating all these variations in species. He wrote down his thoughts in secret notebooks and was only prompted to make his ideas public when he realized that another naturalist, Alfred Russel Wallace, might publish before him. In 1859, Darwin published his theory of evolution in his now famous book, *On the Origin of Species by Means of Natural Selection.*

The mechanism Darwin uses to explain the evolution of species is called natural selection. According to this theory, variations arise randomly in the offspring of animals. Some of these variations enhance an organism's chances of survival in a particular environment, increasing its rate of reproductive success. Such variations are therefore preserved in the population of that species, and those variations that do not enhance survival are weeded out through the competition for

THE ORIGIN OF SPECIES

BY MEANS OF NATURAL SELECTION,

OR THE

PRESERVATION OF FAVOURED RACES IN THE STRUGGLE FOR LIFE.

By CHARLES DARWIN, M.A.,

FELLOW OF THE ROYAL, GEOLOGICAL, LINNÆAN, ETC., SOCIETIES; AUTHOR OF 'JOURNAL OF RESEARCHES DURING H. M. S. BEAGLE'S VOYAGE ROUND THE WORLD.'

LONDON:
JOHN MURRAY, ALBEMARLE STREET.
1859.

The right of Translation is reserved.

"The book that shook the world." Darwin's On the Origin of Species *sold out its first day of publication, then went through six editions.*

existence. Animals with traits that increase their chances of survival are more likely to pass those traits on to their offspring, resulting in the evolution, or adaptation, of animals over long periods of time. When the animals have changed sufficiently from their ancestors, a new species is formed. Darwin followed *The Origin of Species* with a book called *The Descent of Man* in 1871, which further extended his theory of evolutionary change to the evolution of human beings. British philosopher and sociologist Herbert Spencer (1820–1903) coined the phrase "survival of the fittest" to describe Darwin's work, and this term has stuck until the present day.

In 1848, Darwin was knighted for his scientific accomplishments. Though his theory explained so much, Darwin never explained the mechanisms by which random variations were produced in offspring. The way in which traits were passed on to the new generation, the way in which traits from both parents were combined, and the way in which new traits appeared remained a mystery.

CLUES IN THE CELL

While naturalists were explaining how animals changed over time, parallel developments had been taking place in the field of biology that would ultimately explain the mechanisms by which characteristics were passed from one generation to the next.

Robert Hooke was the first to describe the structure of the cell in 1665. Trained as an artist and educated at Christ Church College at Oxford, Hooke was fascinated by mechanical objects and produced many improvements to existing devices such as air pumps and clocks. One of the things he built for himself was a microscope. In 1665, he published a book called *Micrographia*. In this book, he used his drawing

Published in 1665, Robert Hooke's Micrographia *is considered one of the most significant scientific works ever published, and it established microscopy's role in the advancement of science.*

MICROGRAPHIA:

OR SOME

Physiological Descriptions

OF

MINUTE BODIES

MADE BY

MAGNIFYING GLASSES.

WITH

OBSERVATIONS and INQUIRIES thereupon.

By *R. HOOKE*, Fellow of the ROYAL SOCIETY.

Non possis oculo quantum contendere Linceus,
Non tamen idcirco contemnas Lippus inungi. Horat. Ep. lib. 1.

LONDON, Printed by *Jo. Martyn*, and *Ja. Allestry*, Printers to the ROYAL SOCIETY, and are to be sold at their Shop at the *Bell* in S. *Paul's* Church-yard. MLCLXV.

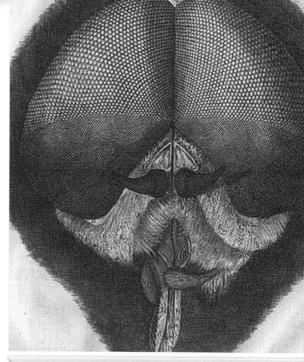

talent to produce pictures of the objects he'd seen with his microscope. His work supported the concept that all living organisms were composed of tiny units called cells and that the working of these cells was responsible for the way that plants and animals functioned.

Robert Hooke's Micrographia *contains stunning detailed illustrations of organisms that cannot be seen with the human eye alone. A fly's eye is one such illustration.*

Caspar Friedrich Wolff (1733–1794), a German biologist working at the St. Petersburg Academy of Sciences in Russia, revived William Harvey's work in support of epigenesis. Wolff took the position that it was some type of particle or germ cell, not tiny preformed people, that produced babies. He proposed that such particles could guide the development of various parts of the body as the embryo grew. Although he couldn't explain how this process worked, he did have the idea that the fertilized egg contained some type of encoded material. In 1759, he wrote his medical school thesis, *Theoria generationis* (A Theory of Reproduction). He stated that embryos of all species go through a continuous series of developmental changes to form the final plant or animal. Furthermore, he claimed that the embryo first consisted of a series of undifferentiated cells that developed into specialized types of tissue and structures. Support for Wolff's theory was provided by the French physician and pathologist Marie-François-Xavier Bichat (1771–1802), who identified twenty-one different types of tissue in the human body. But the process of reproduction and the inheritance of traits still remained a mystery.

3

The Nature
of Inheritance

One of the most pivotal figures in revealing the nature of inheritance was Gregor Johann Mendel. Mendel discovered some of the basic rules that govern inheritance and laid the foundation for our understanding of genetics. Mendel was born on July 22, 1822, in Heizendorf, Austria, the son of Austrian peasants. At the age of twenty-one, he became a friar at an Augustinian monastery in Moravia (now part of the Czech Republic). He was ordained a priest in 1846 and became an abbot in 1868, a post he held until his death in 1884. Mendel also studied chemistry, mathematics, and biology. He had a strong interest in science, and the monastery where he lived had a garden and offered him the time to contemplate what was happening there.

While at the monastery, Mendel crossbred (mated different varieties of) peas and studied the way that the parents' characteristics appeared in their offspring. Among the characteristics that Mendel studied were the height of the pea plants, flower color, pea texture, and so on. Mendel kept a record of his observations in which he recorded the occurrence of key characteristics in the plants he bred. Starting with a single trait, he tracked its occurrence through numerous generations of plants. What he discovered was that a given trait would occur in the daughter pea plants in one of three mathematical ratios: (1) all of the offspring had the same trait as the parent (100 percent), (2) three out of four of the offspring

had the trait (75 percent), or (3) half the offspring had the trait as it appeared in one parent and half had the trait as it appeared in the other parent (50 percent). Mendel got similar results regardless of what type of trait he was studying—flower color (white or purple), smoothness of seed (wrinkled or smooth), or height (tall or short). From this, Mendel concluded that more than chance was operating in the passing on of traits. Some mechanism, he deduced, was obviously responsible for how traits were being passed on. Mendel referred to the elements responsible for transmitting characteristics from parents to children as "genetic factors." This term was later shortened to "gene."

One important feature of Mendel's work was the distinction he drew between phenotype (how something appears when you look at it) and genotype (an internal element that gives an organism the external characteristic). This concept is very important because it proposes that a plant or animal can carry a genetic factor, or gene, that doesn't show in the organism's appearance but that can still be passed on to its offspring, and its offspring can show that characteristic in its appearance. For example, two plants with purple flowers can produce a daughter plant with white flowers. He made a brilliant guess about why this was so.

THE MATHEMATICS OF INHERITANCE

Mendel's observations led him to conclude that the pea plant's characteristics were controlled not by one but by two genes. Based on the ratios he'd documented for the percentage of offspring that would manifest a given trait, he reasoned that organisms carried genes that didn't show up in the appearance of their off-spring. Therefore, some of the genes were stronger than others. For example, the genetic factor for one color of flower (purple) was dominant, or stronger, than the genetic factor for another flower color (white), which was recessive, or weaker. Mendel estab-lished that a given plant would have two factors, or genes, for each characteristic, one gene inherited from each parent. This produced plants of two types.

Homozygous plants are those that have two genes that are the same, and heterozygous plants have inherited two different genes for a given trait. If a plant inherits two of the same genes, they will determine the trait passed on. If a plant inherits two different genes, the one that is dominant will dictate the expression of the trait. For example, if a plant inherits two genes for purple flowers, it will have purple flowers. If it inherits two genes for white flowers, it will have white flowers. If it inherits one gene for purple flowers and one gene for white flowers, it will have purple flowers, because the gene for this color is dominant.

However, a plant that has two different genes can still pass on either one of those genes. If it has two different genes for flower color, it can pass on either a

Though Mendel was unaware of it at the time of his experiments, the simple genetic structure of the pea plant allowed him to obtain absolute results in the plants' inherited traits.

gene for purple flowers or a gene for white flowers. This means that a plant that has two parents with purple flowers can have white flowers if it receives the recessive (white) gene from both its parents. Mendel's theory elegantly accounted for the statistical distribution he observed in the plants he studied. In combining two different genetic factors, there are four possible combinations. One can have purple-purple, purple-white, purple-white again, and white-white. Wherever there is a purple gene, it is dominant and produces a purple flower. This corresponds to the second case discussed earlier, in which 75 percent of daughter pea plants exhibited one dominant trait. In order for the statistical distribution to occur in the manner observed, there had to be an equal chance that a parent would pass on either one of the two genes for a specific characteristic. Thus Mendel's first law, called the law of segregation, states that 50 percent of the sperm or egg cells of a parent carry one of the genes for a specific trait, and 50 percent carry the other gene.

THE NATURE OF INHERITANCE

Mendel's second law, or the law of independent assortment, states that the genes for various characteristics are passed on independently of one another. In other words, the gene for flower color is passed on independently of the gene for wrinkled or smooth peas. A plant with purple flowers could turn out to have either wrinkled or smooth peas, and the same is true for a plant with white flowers. We now know that the law of independent assortment is true only if the genes are on different chromosomes (strands of genetic material composed of genes). Genes on the same chromosome are sometimes related, or linked, and are passed on together. Furthermore, some genes have only partial dominance. When two genes with partial dominance are passed on, the result is an offspring that shows a mixture of the traits seen in the parents. That is why when a black sheep and a white sheep are bred, the resulting lamb may be black, white, or spotted.

Mendel presented his theories to a local society of learned men in Brünn, Moravia, in 1865, but word of his work didn't reach western Europe for some time. The

significance of his work wasn't recognized until German plant geneticist Carl Correns, Dutch botanist Hugo de Vries, and Austrian agronomist Eric Tschermak redis- covered it in 1900. Shortly thereafter, William Bateson, an English zoologist, translated Mendel's work into English and led the effort to promote the study of hered- ity in the United Kingdom.

LOCATING GENETIC MATERIAL

Mendel's work demonstrated that some mechanism was responsible for passing on characteristics from gen- eration to generation in a systematic fashion. However, it was necessary to unlock the secrets of the cell before the nature of that mechanism could be revealed.

In 1833, a Scottish botanist named Robert Brown, working in London, made an observation that shed light on the nature of the cell's structure. Brown was the son of an Episcopalian clergyman. He graduated from Marischal College in Aberdeen, Scotland, and went on

Robert Brown first observed what came to be called Brownian motion: the erratic motion of pollen grains in water caused by the grains themselves.

to study medicine at Edinburgh University, although he did not graduate. Instead, at the age of twenty-one, he joined the Fifeshire Regiment as a surgeon's mate, and while posted in Ireland, he became interested in botany. On a visit to London in 1798, he met Sir Joseph Banks (1743–1820), president of the Royal Society, who was also a botanist. Banks recommended Brown for the post of naturalist aboard the *Investigator,* which was set to go on a surveying expedition along the coast of Australia. During the next

two years, he collected thousands of samples of plants as the *Investigator* circled the continent of Australia. When he returned to England, he devoted himself to classifying the specimens he'd returned with, recording many new species of plant life, and he was eventually appointed to head the botany department at the British Museum.

In 1831, while studying plant cells, Brown noticed the existence of a round, opaque area in the center of the orchid cells he was studying. He called this area the nucleus. A few years later, in 1838, two German scientists and friends, Dr. M. J. Schleiden (1804–1881) and Dr. Theodor Schwann (1810–1882), revealed the importance of the nucleus. Schleiden, a professor of botany at the University of Jena, explained the role of the nucleus in cellular functioning. Building on the work of Brown, Schleiden was convinced that the nucleus was the most important part of the cell. In 1838, he proposed that it was the structure from which all cells developed. He mentioned his ideas to a friend of his, Dr. Theodor Schwann, who was a professor of physiology at the University of Louvain in Belgium.

Schwann, a cytologist, had studied medicine at the University of Berlin under Johannes Müller, who taught many nineteenth-century German physiologists. Schwann, an expert with the microscope, thought that the nucleus Brown had observed in plant cells was the same as the opaque structure he had observed in animal cells. Schwann and Schleiden jointly came up with the theory that cells are the components from which all living things are made. Although they were correct in saying that all living things are made up of cells, they were wrong in thinking that cells built up organisms in a manner similar to the way crystals form. They were, however, correct about the central role that the nucleus plays in controlling cellular processes.

In 1869, a twenty-five-year-old Swiss chemist, Friedrich Miescher (1844–1895), isolated a chemical compound found in the cell's nucleus. He called this

substance "nuclein" because he found it in the nucleus of cells. The significance of his discovery would not be apparent for another seventy years. Today, we call this substance DNA, which stands for deoxyribonucleic acid.

The process of mitosis, or cell division, was identified for the first time in 1882 when German anatomist Walther Flemming (1843–1905), studying cells under a microscope, observed threadlike structures that absorbed the dye he was using to bring out the details of structure in the nucleus. Because the dye he used was called chromatin, Flemming called the stringlike objects he observed in the nucleus "chromosomes." The word is still used to describe the long strings of DNA that carry genetic information.

Mitosis is a process during which the pairs of chromosomes found in the nucleus duplicate themselves, followed by division of the parent cell into two daughter cells, each of which has a complete set of chromosomes. This is reproduction by simple cell division and produces mostly identical cells.

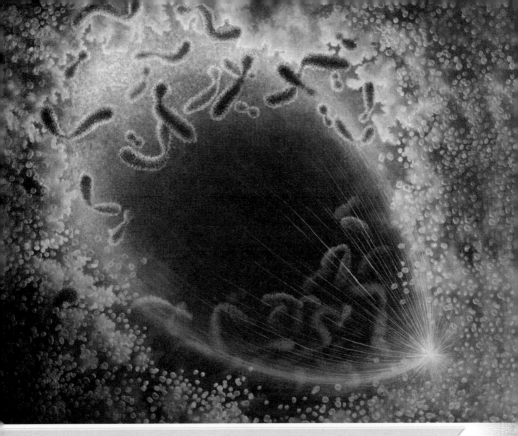

Here, an illustration of mitosis shows chromosomes migrating to opposite ends of the nucleus as it prepares to divide into two daughter cells.

With organisms that reproduce sexually, a different process occurs within the nucleus. This is called meiosis. Here the chromosomes do not duplicate themselves, and when the cell divides, each daughter cell gets only half as many chromosomes as the parent

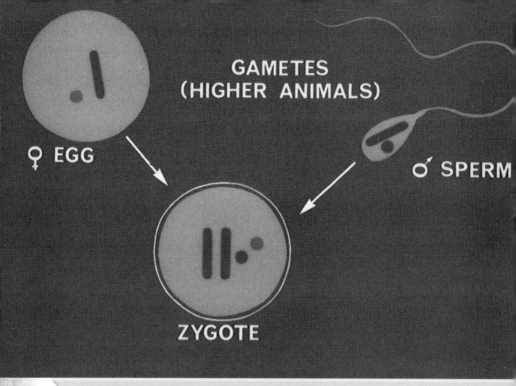

GAMETES
(HIGHER ANIMALS)

♀ EGG

♂ SPERM

ZYGOTE

This is an illustration of how the genetic information is passed along in fertilization. The haploid gametes (egg and sperm) combine to form a diploid individual (zygote).

cell. In this way, sperm and egg cells are formed that each contain only half of the chromosomes found in the cells of a normal animal. When the sperm and egg cells later combine and an embryo is formed, the embryo receives half of its chromosomes from the sperm cell and half from the egg cell. This gives the embryo its own complete pairs of chromosomes, half containing genetic information from its mother and half containing genetic information from its father. In this way, genes are mixed and there is a greater chance for variation in the traits of the daughter organism. With meiosis, daughter cells are not identical to their parent cells.

The Secrets of Genetic Structure

4

The twentieth century was truly the century of the gene. During this century, scientists came to understand the exact nature of DNA and learned how to alter and replace genes to cure illnesses and create new biological organisms. We have decoded the entire structure of the human genome, and we are rapidly learning which genes are responsible for particular human traits. The first step on this journey was to discover the exact nature of genes and chromosomes.

In 1905, Nellie Stevens and Edmund Wilson proposed that separate X and Y chromosomes determine the gender of offspring. This idea was based on the observation that throughout the many different species studied, females always had two chromosomes that were the same (XX) and males always had two different chromosomes (XY).

An interesting fact about the difference in genes between males and females was discovered by Thomas Hunt Morgan (1866–1945), descendant of a distinguished Southern family and graduate of Johns Hopkins University in Baltimore, Maryland. Morgan went to Columbia University in New York City and studied genetics in fruit flies, which are often used in biological research because they are small, easy to raise in a laboratory, have only four chromosomes, and are prolific—that

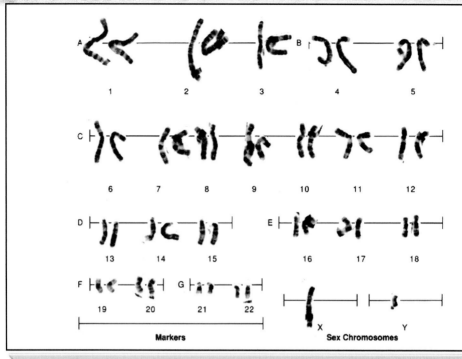

A karyotype of human chromosomes allows scientists to distinguish each set by its size and banding pattern. Each of the trillions of human cells, with few exceptions, contains a complete set of chromosomes.

is, they multiply rapidly and in great numbers. In 1911, after years of breeding fruit flies in the hope of generating a spontaneous mutation, he got a fly with white eyes instead of the normal red eyes most fruit flies have. He bred the white-eyed fly to a red-eyed fly. The result was three red-eyed flies to every white-eyed fly. So far, so good, as far as Mendelian inheritance was concerned. Then he bred the next generation. Unexpectedly, all the white-eyed flies were male. Morgan had discovered the existence of sex-linked genes.

Sex-linked genes are genes that are located on the X and Y chromosomes, and those that are on the Y chromosome are only inherited by males. The gene for white eye color is recessive. This means that a female, who gets two X chromosomes (one from each parent), would have to get two copies of the gene in order to have white eyes. On the other hand, male flies have one X chromosome and one Y chromosome. If the Y chromosome did not have a gene for eye color, then whatever gene (red or white) the fly received from its mother on the X chromosome would determine its eye color. It would therefore be much easier for male flies to have white eyes. In time, Morgan found that several traits were commonly found together on male flies. From this, he concluded that

GENETICS AND EUGENICS

Knowledge can be used for ill as well as good. The new discoveries in the field of genetics led to a new eugenics movement. The term "eugenics" was coined by Francis Galton (1822–1911), a cousin of Charles Darwin. An anthropologist, Galton was interested in studying human intelligence. He was a pioneer in applying statistical methods to biological studies. He wanted to improve the mental and physical characteristics of human beings through selective breeding. Galton believed that people were successful in life entirely because of hereditary factors. He refused to believe that environmental factors played any role in the course of human life. Galton felt that those who had the best genetic characteristics—physical or mental—should be encouraged to reproduce, and those who were "unfit" (for example, the poor and the nonwhite peoples whose cultures he judged inferior) should be discouraged from breeding. In the years prior to World War I

(1914–1917), sixteen states enacted laws for mandatory sterilization (rendering people unable to have children). These laws were aimed at reducing the number of children born to those who were considered "genetically inferior." The "science" of eugenics reached its peak in Nazi Germany's attempt to achieve racial purity by killing millions of Jews and others deemed to be racially impure.

they were all on the male sex chromosome. However, occasionally these "linked" characteristics would be found separately. From this, he concluded that it was possible for pairs of chromosomes to exchange genes, a process called chromosome recombination. One of the principles that Morgan discovered is that the closer two genes are on a chromosome, the more likely it is that they will be linked and the less likely it is that recombination will occur.

GENES AND CHROMOSOMES

In 1913, one of Morgan's students at Columbia, Alfred Sturtevant (1891–1970), realized that if one had a great enough number of mutations, it should be possible to use the strength of linkages as a measure of how far apart on the X or Y chromosome various genes are. This allowed him to make a rough map of where some genes were located on the male and female chromosomes. His idea that genes were lined up along the threadlike chromosomes opened up the possibility of gene mapping. This idea of mapping the locations of genes on chromosomes would reach its peak nearly 100 years later with the Human Genome Project. In 1933, Morgan was awarded the Nobel Prize in Physiology or Medicine for his work with chromosomes.

Hugo de Vries (1848–1935), one of the scientists responsible for reviving Mendel's work at the turn of the twentieth century, also identified the significance of one of the characteristics of inheritance that Mendel had observed in his studies. Every once in a while, Mendel found that a plant produced a completely new characteristic. De Vries identified these sudden changes as genetic mutations. The idea that sudden new characteristics could appear and that organisms could in turn pass them on to their offspring was powerful support for Darwin's theory of evolution. Darwin's theory of natural selection elegantly explained how the environment favors the survival of certain traits, but how those new traits arose was a question that Darwin had left unanswered. Now it was understood that there was a pool of genes that was constantly being reshuffled to create organisms with varying combinations of traits and that sometimes those genes were altered somehow, passing on traits that had never manifested themselves before.

Another of Thomas Hunt Morgan's students at Columbia was Hermann Joseph Muller (1890–1967). Muller also performed experiments using fruit flies, and he demonstrated that a mutation in one gene can change

the way that another gene acts, thus demonstrating that some genes interact with each other. For example, a gene may control whether or not another gene is "turned on," that is, whether it is active and able to manifest itself. This is a principle that would be important to later scientists working in fields like cancer research. It would be found, for example, that a gene that controls cell growth can be held in check by a second gene that inhibits cell growth. If this second gene is removed or suppressed, the first gene may trigger uncontrolled cell growth that results in a tumor.

By 1927, Muller had achieved renown for using X-rays to cause mutations in genes. He warned against the danger of using X-rays in medical treatments that were popular at the time because of the danger of causing genetic mutations, but his warnings were largely ignored

Hermann Muller, here at work on an experiment with fruit flies and radiation, used his publicity as a Nobel Prize winner to warn against the dangers that industrial progress and radiation posed in the form of genetic mutations.

by the medical community of the day. An avid Socialist, Muller was put under surveillance by the FBI. In 1932, he moved to Europe. Muller was awarded the Nobel Prize in Physiology or Medicine in 1946.

Along with the recognition that genes could affect each other, the idea that genes could be transferred from one organism to another would be key in the development of genetic technology in the latter half of the twentieth century. It was Fred Griffith, a British medical officer, who accidentally discovered this fact in 1928. At the time, Griffith was studying the pneumonia bacteria responsible for an epidemic in London. He injected mice with a strain of live but non-lethal *Streptococcus* pneumoniae type I and heat-killed *Streptococcus* pneumoniae type II, which is dangerous and often fatal. Despite the fact that the live bacteria were safe and the lethal bacteria were dead, and therefore couldn't act on the mice's bodies, many of the mice died. When he took samples from the dead mice, Griffith found live, lethal bacteria. Somehow the genetic information from the dead lethal bacteria had been transferred to the live bacteria. His work laid the foundation for molecular genetics and approaches to genetic therapies that depend on the transfer of genes from one cell to another.

Just what was the genetic material made of? This question would be answered by Phoebus Levene (1869–1940). Levene was born in Sagor, Russia, and studied medicine at the Imperial Military Medical Academy. However, anti-Semitism was rampant in Russia, so in 1891, his family moved to the United States, where Levene practiced as a doctor on the Lower East Side of New York City. He continued to pursue biochemical research as well at Columbia University and later at the Rockefeller Institute of Medical Research. There, in 1929, a year after Fred Griffith made his discovery, Levene discovered the chemical compound that makes up chromosomes—deoxyribonucleic acid (DNA). Its exact chemical structure, however, and how it duplicated itself in the reproductive process, was not yet known.

Before scientists could transfer genes around at will, they required a knowledge of how genes could

naturally move from one chromosome to another. Barbara McClintock (1902–1992) was one of the key researchers in the area of gene transposition. Gene transposition occurs when a piece of one chromosome is exchanged with a piece of another chromosome. This

This 1983 photograph of Barbara McClintock was taken at a press conference announcing she had won the Nobel Prize.

exchange of genetic material is called recombination.

After five years of research at Cornell University, in 1931, McClintock and co-researcher Harriet Creighton reported their observation that genetic material could be exchanged between chromosomes in corn. Later, McClintock continued her research at the University of Missouri. While there, she observed that damaged chromosomes could repair themselves.

THE SECRETS OF GENETIC STRUCTURE

While working as an assistant professor of genetics at the University of Missouri in 1940, she was warned by the chairman of the department that she would be fired if she married. This was not an unusual attitude at the time. Many people believed that women just worked until they could find a husband.

Believing that her opportunities for advancement would be limited at the University of Missouri, McClintock left to work at the Department of Genetics at the Carnegie Institution of Washington, located in Cold Spring Harbor, New York, where she spent the next twenty-six years. She continued her research into how genes functioned. She was one of the pioneers in establishing ways that genes were controlled and turned on and off by other genes. The discoveries she made in the field of genetics were key to our understanding of how genes function. She was awarded the Nobel Prize in Physiology or Medicine in 1983. She was the first woman to win an unshared Nobel Prize in this area.

5

Cracking the Genetic Code

In 1941, George W. Beadle (1903–1989) and Edward L. Tatum (1909–1975) threw fresh light on exactly how genetic information was encoded and how that information resulted in the creation of enzymes that helped to form proteins and control the development of the embryo. Beadle and Tatum did much of their work with fruit flies. By

1935, they had produced evidence that eye color in the flies was the result of chemical reactions that were prompted by genes. However, the fruit fly was too complex an organism to reveal links between specific genes and their related chemicals.

The two scientists turned to a bread mold called *Neurospora crassa.* This mold has only one pair of chromosomes, so any mutation or change in the gene sequence is easily spotted. They treated the mold with ultraviolet light to produce a mutation. This particular mutation resulted in offspring that would not reproduce unless a specific amino acid (a chemical that forms proteins), arginine, was added to the medium in which the mold was grown. This indicated that the gene responsible for synthesizing the enzyme that helped to create arginine had mutated and no longer functioned properly. The resulting mutation was passed on to the next generation of mold organisms with the expected Mendelian statistical distribution. This established that instructions for the production of this enzyme was encoded in one gene. Proof of the

concept "one gene, one protein" is key to genetic manipulation because it means that by changing a single gene one can change the protein that is, for example, responsible for a certain medical ailment. Beadle and Tatum established that individual genes encode (carry the pattern for) individual proteins. In 1958, Beadle and Tatum were awarded the Nobel Prize in Physiology or Medicine.

Scientists in the early twentieth century had succeeded in producing mutations artificially through the application of X-rays or ultraviolet light. However, it was not until 1943 that it was demonstrated scientifically that mutations could occur spontaneously without direct exposure to radiation. In that year, Salvador Luria (1912–1991) and Max Delbrück (1906–1981) proved that genetic mutations occur spontaneously in nature— without exposure to radiation or chemicals. That natural changes to genetic material occurred was theorized as early as the second half of the nineteenth century. In fact, it was a pillar of Darwinian theory. But

Dr. George W. Beadle (far left) *and Dr. Edward L. Tatum* (second from left) *pose with five other recipients of Nobel Prize awards on December 10, 1958. Their "one gene, one protein" concept described how each gene determined an enzyme's structure, which in turn allowed for a very specific chemical reaction.*

proving it and demonstrating the mechanism behind it was another story. Luria and Delbrück used bacteria to demonstrate this. When colonies of bacteria are grown in culture media (a gel or liquid that provides nutrients) to which toxic bacteriophages (viruses that infect bacteria) are added, the bacteria die off. After a while,

however, colonies of bacteria start to grow again, and these bacteria are resistant to the viruses that killed off the original colony.

Luria and Delbrück wondered whether this reappearance of the bacteria occurred because some of the bacteria in the original colony had been resistant to the viruses all along or whether in the course of reproduction a genetic mutation occurred in the offspring bacteria that made them resistant to the viruses. They devised an experiment in which they grew a number of different colonies of bacteria, each the offspring of only a few cells. When the colonies were large enough, they added viruses and saw how many bacteria survived in each culture. If there were a few naturally resistant bacteria in each culture, then all the cultures should show similar survival rates of a small number of bacteria. However, if resistance was the result of a mutation, most cultures would have few survivors, but the culture in which the mutation occurred would show a very large number of surviving bacteria. The latter situation turned out to be the case. Thus they demonstrated that resistance to the bacteriophage was the result of a spontaneous mutation. Changes in the genes responsible for specific characteristics arise spontaneously, and organisms with those changes that are most adaptive survive and produce offspring, thus changing the species over time. They were awarded the Nobel Prize in Physiology or Medicine in 1969.

DNA AND GENETIC TRANSMISSION

In 1944, Oswald Avery, Colin MacLeod, and Maclyn McCarty performed critical experiments demonstrating that DNA is responsible for the transmission of genetic information. Avery, MacLeod, and McCarty set up experiments using the pneumococcus bacteria. They combined a nonfatal strain of the *Streptococcus pneumoniae* bacteria with DNA and RNA (ribonucleic acid) from a lethal strain. As in Fred Griffith's earlier experiments with pneumonia bacteria, some lethal

bacteria were produced as the result of the genetic material being transferred from the dead lethal bacteria to the live nonlethal bacteria. When they added RNase, an enzyme that destroys RNA, to the solution, they found that some lethal bacteria were present in the solution, but when they added DNase, an enzyme that breaks down DNA, no lethal bacteria were found, indicating that it was DNA that was responsible for transferring genetic information.

Much of the scientific world remained skeptical, however, until their work was confirmed by Alfred Hershey (1908–1997) and Martha Chase (1930–2003) in 1952. Hershey and Chase used a bacteriophage to prove DNA's role in transmitting genetic information. A bacteriophage is a bacteria-destroying virus, and a virus is basically no more than a central core of DNA surrounded by a protective protein layer. When a bacteriophage infects a cell, it takes over the host cell's internal mechanisms and transfers its own DNA to the cell's nucleus in order to produce more copies of itself.

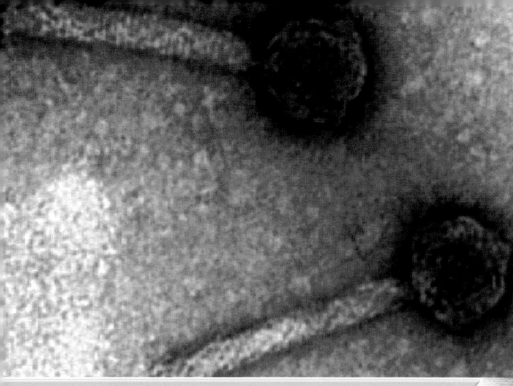

Bacteriophages are made up of a capsid, which holds the virus's nucleic acid, and a protein tail, which recognizes the specific type of bacteria upon which to attach and insert the capsid's genetic material.

Hershey and Chase made radioactive bacteriophages by growing them in culture media that contained radioactive phosphorous. When these radioactive bacteriophages were added to a culture of non-radioactive bacteria, the culture contained bacteria with radioactive phosphorous in their DNA and radioactive sulfur in their proteins. This indicated that when the

bacteriophages had infected the bacteria, they transferred their DNA to the nuclei of the bacteria, and thus DNA was responsible for the transfer of genetic information. In this way, Hershey and Chase confirmed that DNA is indeed the material transferred between cells that controls genetic information. Hershey was awarded the Nobel Prize in Physiology or Medicine in 1969 along with Luria and Delbrück.

In 1950, Erwin Chargaff demonstrated that DNA is composed of four basic proteins, or bases. The particular arrangement of these bases along the strands of DNA is the gene structure and provides the code for the proteins produced by the genes. The four types of bases are adenine (A), thymine (T), cytosine (C), and guanine (G). In 1950, Chargaff, an Austrian immigrant working at Columbia University, discovered that in DNA the amounts of A and T were always equal and the amount of C and G were always equal. He noted, however, that the ratio of A/T to C/G was different in different organisms. This indicated that some type of base pairing, or connection, existed between A and T and between C and G. However, Chargaff could not establish the structure of the pairing.

UNWINDING THE DOUBLE HELIX

It remained for James Watson (1928–) and Francis Crick (1916–) to describe the structure of the base pairing when they explained the entire structure of DNA. James Watson was born in Chicago. In 1952, he went to the world-famous Cavendish Laboratory in Cambridge, England, where X-ray crystallography was being used to study the molecular structure of various biological compounds. Maurice Wilkins (1916–) and Rosalind Franklin (1920–1958) were two scientists working on such projects. At Cambridge, Watson met Francis Crick, an English graduate student writing his dissertation on the application of X-ray crystallographic techniques to the structure of hemoglobin, a constituent of blood.

Watson and Crick were both interested in the structure of DNA. They tried to work out the structure of DNA by building three-dimensional models. They

worked closely with Maurice Wilkins, who supplied them with data produced by Rosalind Franklin, an expert in the new field of X-ray diffraction. In X-ray diffraction, X-rays are bounced off a material, and the resulting pattern on film shows the

James Watson (left) *and Frances Crick demonstrate their model of DNA soon after its discovery in 1953, at their Cambridge laboratory.*

arrangements of molecules. In 1953, using the X-ray diffraction data, Watson and Crick were able to deduce the structure of DNA and construct a three-dimensional model that was in the shape of a double helix, that is, two long strands that twisted around each other like the structure of a spiral staircase. The two strands of DNA are held together by various combinations of the four different bases, like the steps of the spiral staircase. The base adenine (A) on one strand of DNA always bonds with a thymine (T) base on the other strand, and the same is true of the cytosine (C) and guanine (G) bases. Thus Watson and Crick's model explained why there was always the same amount of A and T, and C and G in DNA.

Maurice Wilkins and Rosalind Franklin continued to work with X-ray diffraction, applying the technology to reveal the structure of other biological compounds. Rosalind Franklin died in 1958. Watson eventually became director of the Cold Spring Harbor Laboratory of Quantitative Biology on Long Island, New York, where he spearheaded research in molecular biology. In 1968, when the National Institutes of Health established the National Center for Human Genome Research with the goal of sequencing the entire human genome, Watson became its first director, a position he held until 1992.

Crick continued his genetic research at Cambridge. He and Sydney Brenner established that

every group of three sequential bases on a strand of DNA provides the code for one of the twenty amino acids, or basic proteins, that make up all the tissue in the human body. After spending twenty years at Cambridge, Crick accepted a position at the Salk Institute for Biological Studies in La Jolla, California. In 1962, Watson and Crick and Wilkins were awarded the Nobel Prize in Physiology or Medicine for their work.

The Biotechnology Era

6

Once the structure of DNA was at last revealed, a new era of biotechnology began. Discoveries followed one another quickly. Researchers closed in on their ultimate goals, to be able to remove specific genes from DNA and add new ones, to change the DNA in plants, animals, and, ultimately, people.

One area that scientists focused on was how the proteins in cells were created from the information encoded in genes. The problem was that protein creation occurs in the body of the cell, in organs called ribosomes, not in the nucleus. So it was clear that some other factor was necessary for the process to take place, to transfer the protein-making instructions trapped in the DNA inside the nucleus to the cell body. This transfer agent turned out to be RNA (ribonucleic acid).

Synthesizing DNA itself was another goal. One of the first breakthroughs in creating artificial DNA came in 1958 when two biochemists, Arthur Kornberg (1918–) and Severo Ochoa (1905–1993), working at the National Institutes of Health, isolated an enzyme called DNA polymerase I. This enzyme is responsible for controlling the synthesis of DNA. By combining the proteins that make up DNA with the polymerase I enzyme in test

The contributions of Dr. Arthur Kornberg in DNA synthesis led directly to the development of drugs that treat cancer, AIDS, diabetes, and other potentially fatal diseases.

tubes, strands of DNA were created. Scientists could create different types of DNA by using different proteins. This ability to create DNA with particular characteristics is one of the cornerstones of modern biotechnology. Kornberg and Ochoa were awarded the Nobel Prize in Physiology or Medicine in 1959.

The same year that Kornberg and Ochoa were awarded the Nobel Prize, French scientists François Jacob, André Lwoff, and Jacques Monod, working at the Institut Pasteur in Paris, discovered special genes called regulator genes. Instead of synthesizing proteins, regulator genes control the activity of other genes. There are two types of regulator genes in chromosomes: repressors and operands. These regulators turn the activity of other specific genes off and on. The Institut Pasteur team also established that the DNA in the nucleus of bacteria is in the form of a ring, and this ring of DNA can be broken at any point. Subsequently, scientists would break the DNA ring in bacteria and insert other fragments of DNA into the ring to produce DNA with particular characteristics. Jacob, Lwoff, and Monod were awarded the Nobel Prize in Physiology or Medicine in 1965. Jacob also predicted the existence of messenger RNA, or mRNA. Messenger RNA is the key to transferring the pattern from a gene to the cell tissue where that pattern will be used to create a protein. It wasn't until 1961, however, that the relationship between mRNA and DNA was explained.

In 1959, Marshall Nirenberg, working at the National Institutes of Health, started to investigate how RNA works with DNA to produce proteins. Working with Heinrich J. Matthaei, a German researcher, Nirenberg succeeded in constructing strands of mRNA. RNA is similar to DNA except that it contains the base uracil (U) rather than thymine. Like thymine, uracil will form a base pair with adenine. Using their artificially constructed RNA, Nirenberg and Matthaei were able to demonstrate how RNA carries the messages encoded in DNA and directs the combination of amino acids to create proteins. When it's time for synthesis, the double strands of DNA uncurl. This leaves the base pairs on the two strands unconnected. Molecules of mRNA, consisting of bases that are complementary to the exposed base

pairs on the strand of DNA, then attach to the exposed bases. This process is called transcription. The mRNA detaches and goes into the body of the cell. Here, transfer RNA (tRNA) attaches amino acids to the mRNA. This process is called translation. When the amino acids are strung together, a protein is created. For this knowledge to be useful, however, it was necessary to learn which genes encoded which proteins.

BREAKING THE CODE

The first step in the decoding of DNA occurred in 1966 when Marshall Nirenberg, Heinrich Matthaei, and Severo Ochoa demonstrated that each of the twenty amino acids found in the human body is composed of a sequence of three bases. Nirenberg constructed a strand of mRNA consisting only of the base uracil. In doing so, he found that this triple uracil sequence is the code for phenylalanine, one of the amino acids. This was a critical clue in the attempt to crack the genetic code.

THE BIOTECHNOLOGY ERA

In the early 1970s, two related discoveries paved the way for manipulating genes. In 1970, Peter Duesberg and Peter Vogt isolated an enzyme called reverse transcriptase. This enzyme can be used to cut long strands of DNA at specific locations. This made it possible to delete specific genes out of the strands of DNA. In 1973, Stanley N. Cohen and Herbert W. Boyer developed techniques to insert fragments of DNA, within the existing DNA in a cell nucleus, at a specific point. This was the first artificially created "recombinant" DNA. The ability to produce recombinant DNA and insert it into cells theoretically makes it possible to replace defective genes and to treat the genetically inherited diseases they cause. In 1976, with Robert Swanson, Boyer founded Genentech, one of the first biotech companies. Today, many biotech companies exist and are performing research aimed at creating genetic therapies. These treatments are aimed at curing inherited disorders by replacing defective genes with different genes that function

Genetically modified foods are created when a gene from one organism is inserted into the DNA of another organism, a technique known as recombination, to add a new characteristic or trait. So far, most of this work has involved food plants. The bacterium *Bacillus thuringiensis*, for example, produces a chemical that acts like an insecticide. When a gene from this bacterium is inserted into the DNA of corn or cotton plants, the plants produce their own insecticide and require fewer applications of artificial toxic chemicals. But not everyone believes that such crops are safe for human consumption. Crossbreeding such different organisms, as opposed to crossbreeding, for example, different types of pea plants, also raises concerns that new and lethal organisms will be created. In the United States, almost 80 percent of our corn crop is now genetically modified, with seemingly no effects on the humans who consume it, but many European countries are refusing to purchase such food products. The future of this technology is clouded by economic and political issues.

appropriately. While such treatments could be of great benefit, many issues remain, such as what will happen to future generations as the inserted genes are passed on.

In 1984, Alec Jeffries developed the process of genetic "fingerprinting." This is the basis of the DNA testing we hear so much about in criminal cases in the news today. Jeffries's method involved extracting DNA from a biological sample, such as blood, running it through a gel that separates fragments of DNA, capturing the DNA fragments on a nylon membrane, and tagging them with radioactive probes, molecules that bind to the DNA. A radiograph, a type of picture that shows points of radioactive emission, is taken, and the pattern reveals the sequence of genes in the DNA. Similarities in the DNA between two individuals or between two samples (one found at a crime scene and one from a suspect, for example) can be observed. The first use of DNA testing in a court case occurred in England in 1984. The technique was used to demonstrate the relationship between an immigrant from Ghana and her son. The

ability to identify the parent of a child or a suspect who has committed a crime is useful. Some countries are starting to compile databases of DNA samples. The collection of such samples is worrisome to those who are concerned about issues of privacy and the possible misuse of the information in these databases.

THE ISSUE OF CLONING

In 1997, the Scottish scientist Ian Wilmut and his colleagues at the Roslin Institute demonstrated that the cloning of mammals was possible when they cloned Dolly the sheep. In cloning, the nucleus is removed from the egg cell of an animal. The nucleus of a cell from the animal to be cloned is inserted in place of the removed nucleus. The egg is then inserted into a surrogate mother and allowed to develop. Although Dolly was initially healthy, she seemed to have the genes of a mature sheep, not a young one, and within a few years she developed diseases of old age, such as arthritis. As animals age, mutations occur in genes

Dr. Ian Wilmut, who cloned Dolly, has a vision to create genetically engineered farm animals that can produce proteins in their milk with therapeutic value to humans. He does not embrace the idea of cloning humans and considers being born unique as every child's birthright.

and other elements called telomeres. Many scientists believe that telomeres control how many times a cell can duplicate itself. As more and more cells stop replicating themselves, body tissues become weaker. Some scientists think that this is the process responsible for aging. Such problems demonstrate that although we have the technology to produce clones,

89

Dolly was a carbon copy of her mother, produced from cells in the cloned sheep's mammary gland. Dolly died in February 2003 from a progressive lung disease.

there are many problems with this technology that still need to be resolved. Although there is currently a ban on human cloning in the United States and Europe, countries in other parts of the world, such as Korea, are pursuing research in this area.

On February 11, 2004, in Seoul, South Korea, researchers successfully cloned a human embryo and extracted its stem cells. This is considered a major step in developing cures for diseases such as Parkinson's and diabetes.

THE HUMAN GENOME PROJECT

In order to change the genes in our cells, it is first necessary to establish the code, or sequence of bases, for each gene on each chromosome and to determine what traits each gene controls. This process was made possible by the development of gene sequencing. Fred Sanger, working at the University of Newcastle in England, developed the first DNA sequencing technology in 1977. Sanger used a chemical technique in which he added strands of DNA to be sequenced to four different test tubes, each of which contained a chemical that inhibited one of the four bases (A, G, C, T). When he completed the chemical processing, each of the tubes contained strands whose gaps corresponded to the locations of the base that had been inhibited. This process was labor-intensive and time-consuming, but researchers believed that in time they would sequence all the DNA in human chromosomes.

OWNERSHIP OF MODIFIED GENES

Another area of controversy surrounding genetic engineering and the creation of new organisms is the issue of what lawyers call intellectual property. Who owns such organisms, and who can patent their DNA and prevent others from using such scientific discoveries? Genetic research is very expensive, and usually only governments and large private corporations can afford the investment. Will such discoveries be monopolized by a few large biotechnology corporations? Will the poorer developing nations have to pay exorbitant sums for the cures for genetic diseases discovered by such research? Already such issues have arisen regarding the distribution of expensive AIDS drugs to the poorer African nations. How much is fair compensation to the companies that develop new genetic products, and how long should their patents on such products last? Can anyone own the formula for living organisms?

THE BIOTECHNOLOGY ERA

The Human Genome Project was started in 1988 in the United States. James Watson was recruited to head the new organization responsible for the effort, which was called the National Center for Human Genome Research. It was a $3 billion effort to map and sequence the entire structure of human DNA. The original target date was 2005. Watson remained director of the project until 1992, when he left because the government had started to apply for patents on the gene sequences that were being uncovered. These patents would allow the government to charge a fee for any product produced by a biotech company that used the sequences. Watson felt that it was inappropriate to patent these sequences.

The process of sequencing the human genome went a great deal faster than expected. One major reason for this was the development in the mid-1990s of automated methods of gene sequencing. In 1998, a corporation called Celera Genomics was founded by the Applera Corporation and Dr. J. Craig Venter. Celera Genomic's goal was to sequence the human genome in three years, before the Human Genome Project was

scheduled to complete its work. As a result of this competition and due to improvements in technology, instead of taking until 2005, the work was completed in 2000. The successful sequencing of the human genome was jointly announced by J. Craig Venter and Francis Collins, who had replaced James Watson. The map of the entire human genome was published in 2001 in two journals: *Nature* and *Science*.

This is not the end of the story. Though we know the sequence of bases, it still remains to work out what the different genes do and how they interact with each other. This will not be an easy task. Much more data must be gathered, and complex experiments—not all of which can be conducted in a laboratory setting—must be worked out to link specific genes or combinations of genes to specific human behaviors. There are difficult ethical issues involved in human testing, as well. However, much progress has already been made in identifying the genetic causes of certain diseases and in identifying specific genes, in many different species, that control embryonic development.

THE BIOTECHNOLOGY ERA

Work in genetics during the 1990s paved the way for DNA testing, gene therapy, genetically modified foods, and the possibility of lengthening the human life span. All of these areas represent both opportunities and dangers. The twenty-first century is likely to see a variety of new discoveries and new applications of genetic technology. How shall we use the knowledge we will gain? What will we discover about the relationship between genetically caused characteristics and the influence of our environment on human development? Can we make smarter human beings through gene therapy, or is intelligence a product of many complex factors? Could our experiments create deadly new diseases? Such questions have led to a whole new field of inquiry known as bioethics. Clearly, scientific discoveries in the field of genetics have implications for all of us that are just as serious and dramatic as the discoveries that led to the development of nuclear weapons. It is important that ordinary citizens keep up with the scientists in evaluating the benefits and risks of future discoveries.

Glossary

bacteriophages Viruses that infect and kill bacteria.

chromosome A strand of genetic material made up
of DNA and consisting of a series of genes.
Chromosomes contain the genetic information
that is passed from one generation to the next.

crossbreeding The process of deliberately
breeding together different varieties of
plants or animals.

culture medium A gel or liquid containing nutrients
that allows cells to grow.

cytologist A scientist who studies cells.

deoxyribonucleic acid (DNA)   The substance that makes up chromosomes.

DNase   An enzyme that breaks down DNA.

dominant gene   A gene that will always result in an offspring showing a specific characteristic.

enzyme   A substance that controls a chemical process.

epigenesis   Development of an embryo through a series of steps.

eugenics   The effort to improve human characteristics through selective breeding.

genetic engineering   The process of deliberately altering genes.

heterozygous   Having two genes that are different for a specific trait.

homozygous   Having two genes that are the same for a specific trait.

hybrid   A plant or animal produced by breeding members of two different species.

law of segregation Mendel's first law, which states that 50 percent of the sperm or egg cells of a parent carry one of the genes for a specific trait and 50 percent carry the other gene.

natural selection An evolutionary theory proposed by Charles Darwin whereby animals with traits that enhance their chances of survival pass those traits on to their offspring.

operand genes Genes that turn other genes on.

preformationists Members of a seventeenth-century movement who believed that fully formed miniature beings were carried in their parents' bodies and grew into babies.

probe A molecule that binds to DNA.

recessive gene A gene that will result in an offspring showing a trait only if the offspring receives two copies of the gene, one from each parent.

recombination The exchange of genetic material so that new genes are combined with existing ones.

repressor genes   Genes that turn other genes off.

reverse transcriptase   An enzyme used to cut a gene out of a strand of DNA.

ribonucleic acid (RNA)   A substance that acts as a template for creating proteins encoded in DNA.

RNase   An enzyme that breaks down RNA.

selective breeding   The process of mating two plants or animals in order to produce an offspring with specific traits.

transcription   The process by which a complementary strand of RNA is formed to mirror a strand of DNA.

translation   The process by which amino acids are attached to RNA to form a protein.

transposition   The movement of genes from one chromosome to another.

X-ray diffraction   A process in which X-rays capture patterns on X-ray film to show an arrangement of molecules.

For More Information

ORGANIZATIONS

Human Genome Management Information System
Oak Ridge National Laboratory
1060 Commerce Park MS 6480
Oak Ridge, TN 37830
(865) 576-6669
Web site: http://www.ornl.gov/hgmis

Life Sciences Division
Office of Biological and Environmental Research
Office of Science
ME-2221/Germantown Bldg.

U.S. Department of Energy
1000 Independence Avenue SW
Washington, DC 20585-1290
(301) 903-8521

WEB SITES

Due to the changing nature of Internet links, the Rosen Publishing Group, Inc., has developed an online list of Web sites related to the subject of this book. This site is updated regularly. Please use this link to access the list:

http://www.rosenlinks.com/gsq/gehe

For Further Reading

Asimov, Isaac. *How Did We Find Out About DNA?* New York: Walker, 1985.

Boon, Kevin Alexander. *The Human Genome Project: What Does Decoding DNA Mean for Us?* New York: Enslow Publishers, 2002.

Brookes, Martin. *Get a Grip on Genetics.* New York: Barnes & Noble Books, 2003.

Cefrey, Holly. *Cloning and Genetic Engineering.* Danbury, CT: Children's Book Press, 2002

Jones, Steve, and Borin Van Loon. *Introducing Genetics.* New York: Totem Books, 1998.

Silverstein, Alvin, Virginia Silverstein, and Laura
Silverstein Nunn. *DNA.* New York: Twenty-First
Century Books, 2002.

Snedden, Robert. *DNA and Genetic Engineering.*
London, UK: Heinemann Library, 2003.

Snedden, Robert. *The History of Genetics.* New York:
Thomson Learning, 1995.

Bibliography

DNA Diagnostics Center. "Spiraling Through Genetics History." Retrieved July 2, 2003 (http://www.dnacenter.com/geneticshistory.html).

Evers, Chris. "Legacies: Transformations and DNA." Retrieved July 2, 2003 (http://www.accessexcellence.org/AB/BC/Transformation_and_DNA.html).

Farabee, M. J. *Introduction to Genetics.* Retrieved July 11, 2003 (www.emc.maricopa.edu/faculty/farabee/BIOBK/BioBookgenintro.html).

Federoff, Nina V. "Barbara McClintock." Retrieved July 2, 2003 (http://www.nap.edu/html/biomems/bmcclintock.html).

James Cook University. "Francis Galton: A Exploration in Intellectual Biography and History." Retrieved July 2, 2003 (http://www.maps.jcu.edu.au/hist/stats/galton).

Johnston, Ian. . . . *And Still We Evolve: A Handbook on the History of Modern Science.* Nanaimo, BC: Malaspina University College, 2000. Retrieved July 2, 2003 (http://www.mala.bc.ca/~johnstoi/darwin/sect5.htm).

Kandel, Eric R. "Thomas Hunt Morgan at Columbia University." Retrieved July 2, 2003 (http://www.columbia.edu/cu/alumni/Magazine/Legacies/Morgan).

Kumin, Jochen. "Arthur Kornberg." Retrieved August 19, 2003 (http://www.accessexcellence.org/AB/BC/Arthur_Kornberg.html).

Lasker Foundation. "Albert Lasker Award for Basic Medical Research." Retrieved July 2, 2003 (http://www.laskerfoundation.org/awards/library/1980basic.shtml).

Minnesota State University eMuseum. "Charles Darwin." Retrieved July 2, 2003 (http://emuseum.mnsu.edu/information/biography/abcde/darwin_charles.html).

Minnesota State University eMuseum. "Jean Baptiste Lamarck." Retrieved July 2, 2003 (http://emuseum.mnsu.edu/information/biography/klmno/lamarck_jean.html).

National Health Museum. "Biographies." Retrieved July 2, 2003 (http://www.accessexcellence.org/AB/WYW/wkbooks/SFTS/biography.html).

National Institutes of Health, National Library of Medicine. "The Marshall W. Nirenberg Papers, Biographical Information." Retrieved August 19, 2003 (http://profiles.nlm.nih.gov/JJ/Views/Exhibit/narrative/biographical.html).

Royal College of Physicians. "Sir Archibald Edward Garrod." Retrieved July 2, 2003 (http://www.aim25.ac.uk/cgi-bin/search2?coll_id=7107&inst_id=8).

BIBLIOGRAPHY

Texas Tech University Health Sciences Center.
"William Harvey." Retrieved July 2, 2003 (http://
phy025.lubb.ttuhsc.edu/Figures/Harvey.shtml).

University of California, Berkeley. "Carl Linneaus."
Retrieved July 2, 2003 (http://www.ucmp.berkeley.
edu/history/linnaeus.html).

University of St. Andrews. "Robert Hooke." Retrieved
July 2, 2003 (http://www-gap.dcs.st-and.ac.uk/
history/Mathematicians/Hooke.html).

Whonamedit.com. "Robert Brown." Retrieved July 2,
2003 (http://www.whonamedit.com/doctor.cfm/
2539.html).

Whonamedit.com. "Friedrich Wolff." Retrieved July 2,
2003 (http://www.whonamedit.com/doctor.cfm/
2433.html).

Williams, Henry Smith. "A History of Science."
Retrieved July 2, 2003 (http://anatomy.med.unsw.
edu.au/cbl/embryo/history/page4d.htm).

Index

Credits

ABOUT THE AUTHOR

Jeri Freedman has a B.A. from Harvard University and spent fifteen years working in companies in the biomedical and high technology fields. She is the author of several plays and, under the name Foxxe, is the coauthor of two science fiction novels. She lives in Boston.

PHOTO CREDITS

Designer: Nelson Sá; **Editor:** Leigh Ann Cobb;
Photo Researcher: Nelson Sá